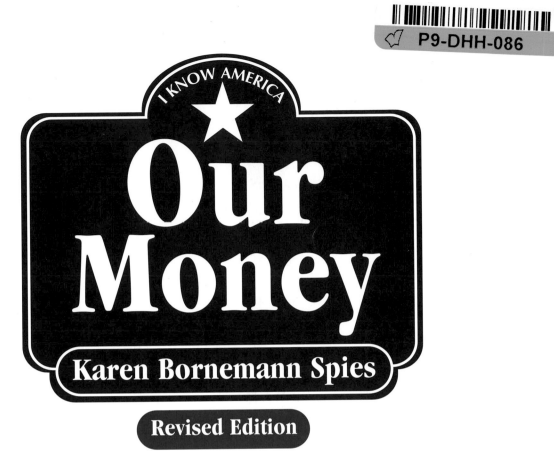

I KNOW AMERICA

Our Money

Karen Bornemann Spies

Revised Edition

THE MILLBROOK PRESS
Brookfield, Connecticut

Cover photographs courtesy of © Tony Freeman/PhotoEdit, AP/Wide World Photos and Ginger Giles

Photographs courtesy of North Wind Picture Archives: pp. 4, 6, 7, 10 (bottom), 13; Library of Congress: pp. 8, 20; © Douglas A. Mudd/Smithsonian Institution, National Museum of American History, National Numismatic Collection: pp. 10 (top), 11 (top), 15; Architect of the Capitol: p. 11 (bottom); National Portrait Gallery, Smithsonian Institution: p. 12; © Richard Glassman: p. 16; © Stuart Rabinowitz: p. 23; Bureau of Engraving and Printing, U. S. Treasury: pp. 26, 33; Official United States Mint Photographs: pp. 31, 32; AP/Wide World Photos: pp. 34, 40; © David Young-Wolff/PhotoEdit: p. 38; Corbis/Bettmann: p. 45

Library of Congress Cataloging-in-Publication Data
Spies, Karen Bornemann.
Our money / Karen B. Spies.
p. cm. — (I know America)
Includes bibliographical references and index.
Summary: A brief history of money in the United States and a description of its minting and use.
ISBN 0-7613-2620-0 (lib. bdg.)
1. Money—United States—History—Juvenile literature. [1. Money—United States—History. 2. Money.] I. Title. II. Series.
HG501.S75 2001
332.4'973—dc21 2001037014

Published by The Millbrook Press, Inc.
2 Old New Milford Road
Brookfield, Connecticut 06804
www.millbrookpress.com

CONTENTS

CHAPTER

THE MEANING OF MONEY

Imagine that you are stranded on a desert island with a million dollars. How much is it worth? You can't eat it. You have nothing to spend it on. Basically, your money has no value. But once you are rescued, your money immediately becomes very valuable. Why? Because it can buy a lot.

How can money be worthless one minute and valuable the next? What is money anyway? Money is an easy way for people to trade one thing for another. Another name for money is *currency*. Currency refers to both coins and paper money.

How did people get things before currency was invented? Mostly, they traded something they had for something else they wanted. This was known as

Opposite: **Coinmakers in the Middle Ages cut and stamped gold and silver to make coins.**

5

This banknote from the Chinese Ming Dynasty is an early form of paper currency.

bartering. For example, let's say a blacksmith made tools and a farmer raised cows. If the farmer needed a tool and the blacksmith wanted a cow, then bartering worked well. But what if the blacksmith wanted a cow, but the farmer didn't need any new tools? Then the blacksmith would have to search for someone else who wanted tools and who had something that the farmer would take for a cow. Bartering became impractical. Besides, it was hard to "make change" with a cow.

Early Kinds of Money

In most early civilizations one or two things came to be used as money. Sometimes, it was a useful item such as salt. In other places, common everyday items that may sound odd today were considered valuable. For example, fishhooks, human skulls or teeth, and feathers have all been used as "money" at one time or another. Until the 1940s, people on the South Pacific islands of Yap used giant round stones as money. The larger the stone, the more it was worth. Some stones were as large as truck tires and weighed more than a hundred pounds!

Gradually, it became common to trade precious metals for goods. Bronze or gold was shaped into crude bars (ingots). Large bronze or gold pieces were worth more than small ones. Unfortunately, it was hard to tell how much more they were worth. Each individual piece had to be weighed one at a time to determine its value.

Eventually, precious metals such as gold and silver were made into small disks, or coins. The earliest known coins were made in Asia Minor (now modern-day Turkey) about 700 B.C. by the people from a region called Lydia.

Paper Instead of Metal

No matter what metals the coins were made of, carrying a lot of them was difficult. Imagine buying a house and paying for it with coins! That is why paper money was invented. It was first used in China in the thirteenth century. After visiting there, the famous explorer Marco Polo reported that the emperor Kublai Khan printed notes on mulberry paper.

Our currency system today still uses a mix of coin and paper money. Many people now also use checks and credit cards to purchase goods and services. Whatever forms of money we use today, they are definitely easier than trading tools for cows.

7

CHAPTER

WAMPUM AND SHINPLASTERS

When European settlers first came to North America, they brought their own coins. However, to trade with the Native Americans, the settlers had to use Native American money—wampum, or tiny shells. Strings of shells were cut into six-foot lengths known as fathoms. An earthenware pot for cooking or storing food was worth one fathom. A good deerskin cost two fathoms. Wampum was legal tender (a lawful form of money) in the colonies until 1701.

Early Colonial Money

Some of the colonies made their own coins. The Massachusetts Bay Colony opened a mint in Boston in 1652. The mint made Pine Tree shillings until 1686.

Opposite:
English explorers traded goods with Indians from the islands of the West Indies.

9

The silver Pine Tree shilling was made in Massachusetts between 1652 and 1686.

The colonists also used foreign gold and silver coins. Great Britain owned the colonies, so British pounds, shillings, and pence were common. Pirates and Spanish explorers used Spanish coins to purchase supplies and luxury goods in the colonies.

The First American Paper Money

American paper money first appeared in 1775. The colonies were fighting with Great Britain. One way to show their independence was to issue their own money. It was known as Continental Currency. The value of this money was backed up by a supply of gold. Since gold is always valuable, it is commonly used to "insure" the value. Unfortunately, the Continental Congress did not have enough coins or gold to back up all the bills it printed. The bills lost their value. That is why colonists said any worthless thing was "not worth a Continental."

Early American paper money from the Revolutionary War

The government stopped making Continental Currency in 1781. But the new nation still needed a national currency system. Members of the Congress wanted American money to be admired and respected throughout the world.

The first national coins were made in 1787. They were copper one-cent coins decorated with a chain of thirteen links. The links circled the words "We Are One." On September 11, 1789, Alexander Hamilton was appointed as the first secretary of the Treasury. Under his leadership, new steps were taken to create public credit for citizens. His reports and many other programs did much to create a sound monetary system for a young United States.

Alexander Hamilton served as the first secretary of the U.S. Treasury.

The Coinage Act

In 1792, Congress passed the Coinage Act. It adopted the dollar as our standard monetary unit. The Coinage

David Rittenhouse served as the first director of the U.S. Mint.

Act also established our country's first mint, located in Philadelphia, to produce coins. The prominent scientist and astronomer David Rittenhouse was appointed as the first director of the U.S. Mint.

The new mint was only a few hundred feet from President Washington's home. The first coins minted were half dimes. They were made from household silver donated by George and Martha Washington. All the new coins showed either a head or full figure of a woman who represented Liberty. This was a symbol of American independence. Most European coins at the time had portraits of kings and queens on

Cabbage, fin, sawbuck. They're all terms for money. What do they mean? Where did they come from?

Buck: A $1 bill. Probably came from the custom of using buckskins as money.

Fin: A $5 bill. Fin is short for finf, the Yiddish word for five.

Greenbacks: Paper money. The term was first used in the Civil War and refers to the green ink used to print the backs of bills.

Hard money: Coins.

Lettuce or cabbage: Paper money. Refers to the green color.

Pin money: Extra cash. Came from the allowance given to women in colonial times to spend on pins. Pins were scarce and expensive. As pins became more plentiful, women spent the money on other things.

Trading with buckskins

Sawbuck: A $10 bill. Related to the use of "buckskins" as money; probably meaning a group of skins or an exceptionally valuable skin.

Shelling out: To pay. Comes from the wampum shells Native Americans used for money.

Soft money: Paper currency. Also called folding money.

Two bits: Slang name for a quarter. *Four bits* is a half dollar. First used in colonial times, when colonists cut Spanish gold coins ("pieces of eight") to make change. Half a coin was "four bits," and a quarter section was "two bits."

them. President Washington did not want his likeness on any American coins. He thought it would look as if he were trying to be a king.

The United States government did not issue paper money until the Civil War. Until then, paper money was printed by private companies and state banks. Pennsylvania alone issued 250 different kinds of bills. Massachusetts had thirteen different kinds. But when the war came, a great deal of money was needed to finance it. So the government began to print "greenbacks." This nickname came from the green ink used to print the back side of the bills. Greenbacks were worth less than their face value (amount printed on the front). In other words, if you turned in a five dollar bill to the government during the Civil War, you would have received less than five dollars worth of gold.

Shinplasters and Confederate Money

Because people hoarded coins, there weren't enough to make change. The government issued tiny bills known as fractional currency. They were about the size of postage stamps. They were printed in denominations of 3 cents, 5 cents, 10 cents, 15 cents, 25 cents, and 50 cents. These small bills were also called shinplasters. Soldiers used them to line their shoes and wrap their shins to keep out the cold.

During the Civil War, the Confederacy issued its own currency as a way to emphasize the strong independence of the Southern states. These notes were good only in states that had seceded, or withdrawn, from the Union.

After the Civil War, the United States was united again under one government. Paper money became more valuable. For every dollar in paper money, the United States owned an equal amount of gold bullion (gold bars). Beginning in 1865, the government began printing paper money known as gold certificates. These certificates could be exchanged for gold bullion. Gold certificates continued to circulate (were in use) until 1933.

Silver certificates were first issued in 1878. They could be exchanged for silver dollars or silver bullion. By the late 1960s, there was a worldwide shortage of silver. For this reason, the government stopped circulating silver certificates in 1968. They were replaced by Federal Reserve notes, which are still in use today.

WHO'S ON A $100 BILL?

Do you know who or what is pictured on each piece of paper money? Can you describe what is stamped on each U.S. coin? This chapter answers these questions.

Current Types of U.S. Bills

There are two kinds of paper money in circulation. Both United States notes and Federal Reserve notes are legal tender for paying bills and debts.

Federal Reserve Notes
Federal Reserve notes make up about ninety-nine percent of all paper money in circulation. They are issued by the Federal Reserve Bank in denominations of $1, $2, $5, $10, $20, $50, and $100. Some $500,

Opposite:
The Federal Reserve Board Building is in Washington, D.C. The Federal Reserve controls the supply of money in the United States.

$1,000, $5,000, and $10,000 bills are still circulated today, but none have been printed since 1945.

United States Notes
United States notes were the country's first national paper currency. They were originally issued in 1862 in these denominations: $1, $2, $5, $10, $20, $50, $200, $500, $1,000, $5,000, and $10,000. Today United States notes make up only a small part of the paper money in circulation. They are issued only in the $100 denomination. At some point, they will no longer be used, since they serve the same purpose as the newer Federal Reserve notes.

What's Printed on Our Paper Money?

Each denomination has a unique portrait of a famous American on the front. Each back also has its own individual design. The $100, $50, $20, $10, and $5 bills have a new design. All bills, however, are printed with certain items in common.

Serial Numbers and Star Notes
Each note has its own eight-digit serial number that appears twice on the face, or front of the note. A serial number includes a letter in front of it and another after it (serial numbers on the new bills have two letters in front and one in back), except for serial numbers on "star" notes. A star note replaces a regular note that has been damaged in printing. It is just like the note it

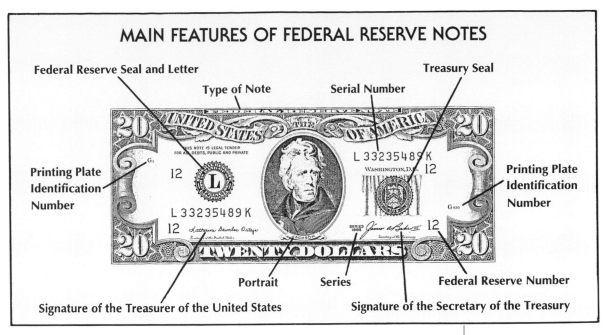

MAIN FEATURES OF FEDERAL RESERVE NOTES

Federal Reserve Seal and Letter · Type of Note · Serial Number · Treasury Seal · Printing Plate Identification Number · Printing Plate Identification Number · Portrait · Series · Federal Reserve Number · Signature of the Treasurer of the United States · Signature of the Secretary of the Treasury

replaces except for the star, which is substituted for one of the serial letters.

Series

All paper money bears a series identification. The series date shows the year in which each bill was reprinted. On bills printed before 1996, the series number is engraved between the portrait and the signature of the secretary of the Treasury. On new bills, the first letter in the serial number shows the series; the letter A stands for 1996.

Treasury Seal

This seal has been on every piece of United States paper money since 1862. It includes a key, which stands for safety, and scales, which stand for justice. The Treasury Seal, or "stamp of approval," shows that the bill is legal tender. It appears in several different forms and colors depending on the bill's denomination.

19

The Great Seal of the United States

The Great Seal was adopted in 1782 and now appears on the back of the $1 bill. The seal shows the bald eagle, our national bird. A shield with vertical stripes and a wide bar across the loop—the arms of the United States—is on its chest. Above the eagle are thirteen stars, which stand for the thirteen original colonies. The eagle holds a ribbon printed with the Latin motto *E pluribus unum* ("Out of many, one"). On the seal back, at the left side of the bill, is an image of an unfinished pyramid, a symbol of strength. Above the pyramid is the "all-seeing eye of God" inside a triangle. At the base of the pyramid are the Roman numerals for 1776, the date of our nation's birthday. Around the edge at the top is a Latin motto, *Annuit coeptis* ("[God] has favored our undertakings"). On a ribbon at the bottom is another bit of Latin: *Novus ordo seclorum* ("A new order of the ages").

The Great Seal appears on many official U.S. items and documents, including the back of the $1 bill.

"In God We Trust"

The motto "In God We Trust" first appeared on coins during the Civil War. However, it was not printed on paper currency until 1957. A determined man named Matt Rothert convinced the government to add the motto to paper money. Rothert wrote more than one thousand letters to government leaders. Finally, his idea became law in 1955.

20

MONEY MATCHES

The following images appear on U.S. bills:

Face (front)   **Reverse (back)**

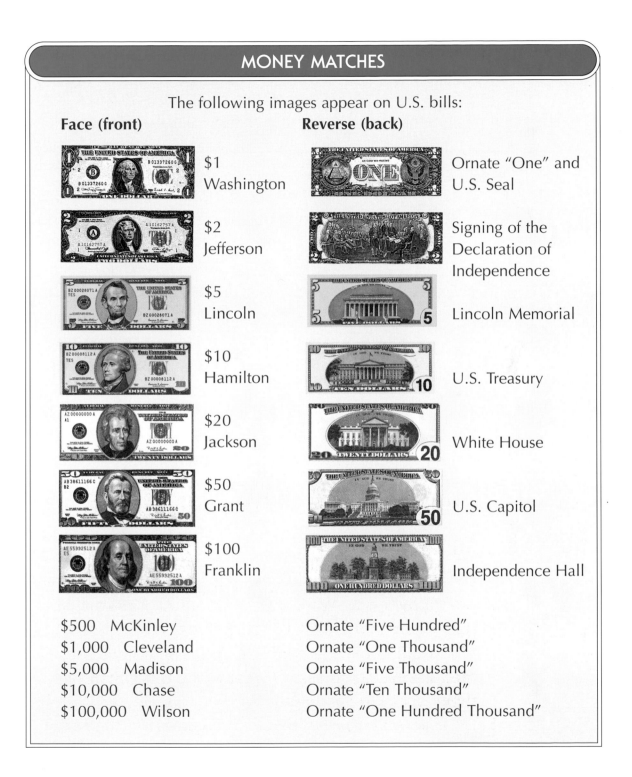

$1 Washington — Ornate "One" and U.S. Seal

$2 Jefferson — Signing of the Declaration of Independence

$5 Lincoln — Lincoln Memorial

$10 Hamilton — U.S. Treasury

$20 Jackson — White House

$50 Grant — U.S. Capitol

$100 Franklin — Independence Hall

$500   McKinley — Ornate "Five Hundred"
$1,000   Cleveland — Ornate "One Thousand"
$5,000   Madison — Ornate "Five Thousand"
$10,000   Chase — Ornate "Ten Thousand"
$100,000   Wilson — Ornate "One Hundred Thousand"

Signatures, Letters, and Numbers

All paper currency shows the engraved facsimile, or copy, of two signatures. Since 1914, all bills show the signatures of the secretary of the Treasury and of the treasurer of the United States. But different bills may have different signatures. That is because many people have served in these positions over the years.

Bills are printed in sheets, thirty-two at a time. Small letters and numbers show each bill's location on the print sheet. These letters and numbers appear on the front of the bill.

CODING OUR CURRENCY

The United States is divided into twelve Federal Reserve districts. Each Federal Reserve bank is in charge of the currency circulation for its district. A seal printed in black at the left of the portrait gives the name and letter of the Federal Reserve bank that issued it. On the new bills, a universal seal is used to represent the entire Federal Reserve system. A letter and number beneath the left serial number identifies the issuing Federal Reserve bank.

The district numbers, cities, and their matching letter symbols are:

1	Boston	A	7	Chicago	G
2	New York	B	8	St. Louis	H
3	Philadelphia	C	9	Minneapolis	I
4	Cleveland	D	10	Kansas City	J
5	Richmond	E	11	Dallas	K
6	Atlanta	F	12	San Francisco	L

U.S. Coins

Many changes in coin design have been made since 1792, when the Mint was founded. At that time, gold was used in the eagle ($10), half eagle ($5), and quarter eagle ($2.50) pieces. The dollar, half dollar, quarter, dime, and half dime were made of silver. The cent and half cent were made of copper.

In 1933, during the Great Depression, the Mint stopped producing gold coins. In 1970, silver was

The secretary of the Treasury chooses the designs for paper currency. The designs must have

historical importance. They cannot depict a living person. Different engravers are chosen to do the portraits, letters, backgrounds, and borders.

The designs on today's bills date from 1929, when all bills were changed to the modern small size. The secretary of the Treasury appointed a committee to decide whose pictures should appear on the bills. The committee thought that all the bills should show United States presidents. The secretary of the Treasury changed the committee's decision slightly. Alexander Hamilton was chosen to be on the $10 bill, because he was the first secretary of the treasury. Benjamin Franklin appears on the $100 bill, because he was a famous statesman and one of the signers of the Declaration of Independence. A picture of Salmon P. Chase was printed on the $10,000 bill. As

secretary of the Treasury during the Civil War, Chase helped develop and oversee the creation of our national banking system.

eliminated from newly minted United States coins. This change was necessary because of the world shortage of silver. Today coins are made of a core of nonprecious metal, such as copper. The core is "clad," or sandwiched between, layers of alloy (two or more metals combined together).

A stack of currency one mile high would contain over 14.5 million notes.

• If you had ten billion $1 bills and spent one every second of every day, it would take 317 years for you to go broke.

• How many times do you think you could fold a dollar bill before it would tear? About four thousand double folds (first forward and then backward) are necessary before a dollar will tear.

• The largest denomination of paper money ever printed was the $100,000 gold certificate of 1934. It was used only in official bank deals. The largest bill printed for circulation was the $10,000 one.

• The Bureau of Engraving and Printing has printed paper currency for the governments of the Philippines, the Republic of Cuba, Thailand, and Korea.

• The Philadelphia and Denver mints regularly produce more than 75 million coins every twenty-four hours.

• The Mint has made coins for China, Costa Rica, El Salvador, Haiti, Honduras, Israel, Liberia, Mexico, and the Philippines.

What's on Each Coin?

Each coin must be stamped with the amount of money it is worth. The word *Liberty* is stamped on coins to remind us that we live in a country that loves freedom. The Latin motto *E pluribus unum* ("Out of many, one") tells that many people joined together to form our nation. The motto "In God We Trust" has appeared on all coins since 1984.

Some coins contain a mint mark. The letter D is stamped on coins from the Denver Mint, a P means Philadelphia, an S stands for San Francisco, and a W means West Point.

Who's on Each Coin?

By law the design of coins cannot be changed more often than once every twenty-five years without the approval of Congress. Most current coins honor U.S. presidents. The Sacagawea, Susan B. Anthony, and American Bald Eagle dollar coins are three exceptions. Quarters honoring the fifty states of the Union were introduced beginning in 1999. The John F. Kennedy half dollar, introduced in 1964, is the most recent coin depicting a president. The Dwight D. Eisenhower dollar is no longer made but is still legal tender.

COINING AN IMAGE

The following images appear on these commonly circulated coins:

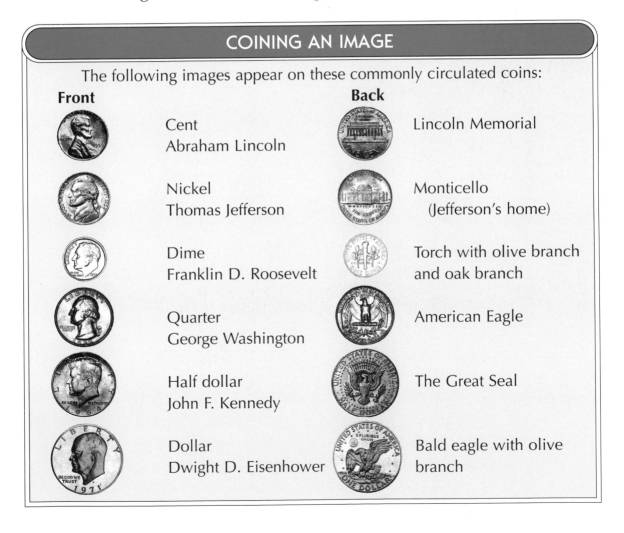

Front

Cent
Abraham Lincoln

Nickel
Thomas Jefferson

Dime
Franklin D. Roosevelt

Quarter
George Washington

Half dollar
John F. Kennedy

Dollar
Dwight D. Eisenhower

Back

Lincoln Memorial

Monticello
(Jefferson's home)

Torch with olive branch
and oak branch

American Eagle

The Great Seal

Bald eagle with olive
branch

MAKING OUR MONEY

The Department of the Treasury has two divisions that prepare all paper money and coins. These divisions are the United States Mint and the Bureau of Engraving and Printing (BEP).

The United States Mint

The headquarters of the U.S. Mint is in Washington, D.C. The coins are made in two branches of the Mint, in Philadelphia and Denver. Commemorative coins are made at the San Francisco Mint in California and at the West Point Mint in New York. Commemoratives honor landmark dates, special people, or events in U.S. history and are very popular among the growing group of coin collectors. The U.S. Bullion Depository, located in Fort Knox, Kentucky, stores the government's vast amount of gold bullion (gold bars, or ingots). Silver bullion is stored at the West Point Mint.

Opposite:
Metal printing plates for a $1 bill cover a press at the Bureau of Engraving and Printing.

27

MONEY TALK

Alloy: A combination of two or more metals.

Annealing: The heating process that softens metal.

Blanks: Circles of metal to be made into coins. See planchet.

Bullion: Bars of crudely prepared metal.

Cladding: The process of bonding strips of metal together. Used today in the making of coins.

Die: A device for exactly copying patterned impressions.

Ingot: A mass of metal cast into a bar shape.

Numismatics: The study or collection of currency.

Planchet: A blank coin.

Upsetting machine: The machine that spins blanks. As it spins, the machine puts the raised edges on the coins.

How Coins Are Made

Before a coin begins production, a design must be approved by the secretary of the Treasury. Once a design is final, a model is made from soft Plasticine (modeling wax). Then a plaster of Paris model is made from the Plasticine one, with most of the details added. The plaster of Paris model is used to make a final model from epoxy, which is a very hard substance. A special tracing tool transfers the design from the epoxy to a metal blank (a coin with nothing stamped on it). Master printing dies are made from the blank. These dies then imprint the words and pictures onto the finished coins.

Let's go on a tour through the Mint and follow the steps in making a coin.

1. A Metal "Sandwich"

Gone are the days of coins made of silver and gold. Today's coins are made of strips of alloy. The strips are shipped to the Mint from private companies. They weigh about six thousand to eight thousand pounds. The strips are 13 inches wide and 1,500 feet long. That's as long as five football fields.

Dimes, quarters, half dollars, and dollars are made of three layers of metal bonded together like a sandwich. This process is called cladding. The top and bottom of the metal "sandwich" is a mixture of three parts copper to one part nickel. The core is pure copper. If you look at the edges of one of these coins, you can see the "sandwich" layers.

Once a coin design is approved, a model of the coin is made from a modeling wax called Plasticine. Then a plaster of Paris model is made from the Plasticine model. An epoxy model is then made from the plaster of Paris version.

Plasticine mold　　　　　　**Plaster of Paris mold**

THE 50 STATE QUARTERS PROGRAM

In December 1997, Congress passed a law called the 50 State Quarters Program Act. Its goal was to encourage young people and their families to learn more about each of the fifty states of the Union.

Beginning in 1999, five new state quarter designs will be issued each year through 2008. Quarters will be produced at both the Philadelphia and Denver mints. Each quarter will be produced in limited quantities every ten weeks.

On one side, the coins will picture George Washington, just like the traditional quarters do. On the reverse side, the coins will bear a design which honors each state and its unique traditions and history. Each quarter will be stamped with the state's birthday. The program has become very popular and encouraged the growth of coin collecting.

The strips for nickels are cupro-nickel—three parts copper and one part nickel. Since 1982, pennies have been made of copper-plated zinc. They are cheaper to manufacture and weigh less than copper cents.

2. The "Cookie Cutter"

The metal sheets are fed into machines called blanking presses. The presses stretch the metal and cut round blanks (planchets). The leftover punched sheets, called "webbing," are melted down and made into new ones.

3. Heat, a Bath, and a Shine

The blanks are heated in a very hot oven called an annealing furnace. This softens them and prepares them for stamping. The softened blanks are put in a chemical bath, which cleans and polishes them. This process is called "pickling." Then the planchets are rinsed and dried.

4. Rolled Rims

This process is like putting the edge on a pizza crust. The blanks go into an "upsetting" machine, which spins like a merry-go-round. The spinning pushes the blanks against the edge of the machine. This produces the raised ("upset") rim.

5. Striking

The planchets are put into a coin press. A ring, or collar, holds each blank in place. Master coinage dies strike, or stamp, the designs onto the blanks. One heavy blow stamps the coins on each side at the same time.

6. Shaking, Counting, and Weighing

The finished coin passes through a "shaker," which vibrates them. The ones that are too small or too large stay in the shaker. The good coins are then counted by machine and put into bags. The bags are sewn shut by a special machine that looks like a handheld sewing machine. The bags are weighed before they are stored or shipped. The scales are so accurate that they can tell if a bag is short only one coin!

Dimes, quarters, half dollars, and dollars are put into sacks that each holds $1,000 worth of coins. Nickels sacks hold $200 each, and cents, $50.

Finished coins are counted and then sewn into bags by a special machine.

The Bureau of Engraving and Printing

All paper money is designed at the headquarters of the Bureau of Engraving and Printing (BEP) in Washington, D.C. About $22.5 million dollars are printed each day in Washington, D.C., and at a branch of the BEP in Fort Worth, Texas. The Bureau also prints Treasury bonds, U.S. postage stamps, and other important documents.

The Engraving Process

Paper money is printed by the intaglio process from engraved plates. First, the different parts of the design are hand-tooled into steel plates. Specially skilled engravers use delicate tools called gravers. For security reasons, each feature on each bill is hand-engraved by a different engraver. Thus, one engraver does the portrait, another does the border, another does the numerals, and so on. Picture engravers must serve as apprentices for ten years before they are allowed to do an actual bill. Letter engravers are apprenticed for seven years.

If you look closely at a bill, you can see the skill and artistry of each engraver. Notice that the portrait is made of many fine lines, dots, and dashes. These vary in size and shape. The use of both heavy and light lines makes counterfeiting (forging or illegal copying of a bill) very difficult.

Early in 2000, the U.S. Mint introduced a gold-colored dollar to replace the Susan B. Anthony dollar. The front side of the coin bears the image of Sacagawea and her baby. Sacagawea was the Native American woman who helped Lewis and Clark on their exploration of the North American continent from 1804 to 1806. The back of the coin bears a soaring bald eagle, our national bird, and seventeen stars. These stars represent the seventeen states that formed the Union at the time of the Lewis and Clark Expedition. Although the coin is nicknamed the Golden Dollar, it does not contain any gold. It is made mostly of copper. The gold-colored metal on the outside of the coin is a manganese-brass alloy.

The next step in the process is transferring the hand-engraved dies to a printing plate. The original engraved dies are stored. They may be used over again.

The Printing Process

The bureau prints all paper money on high-speed printing presses. The most modern presses use four plates of thirty-two bills each. They print over eight thousand sheets per hour. That's more than a quarter of a million bills each hour.

The bills are printed on specially produced paper made from a blend of cotton and linen. The backs of the notes are printed with green ink. They are allowed to dry for twenty-four to forty-eight hours. Then the faces are printed with black ink and allowed to dry.

The intaglio printing process produces notes that have a slightly raised surface. The reverse side feels slightly indented.

Checking, Cutting, and Overprinting

After the printing, each thirty-two-bill sheet is cut in half. It is examined for mistakes. Then a letterpress completes the printing process. The serial number, Treasury seal, and appropriate Federal Reserve district seal and number are printed on the bills.

Special machines cut the notes into individual bills. (Currency printed since 1929 measures 6.14 inches by 2.61 inches.) The bills are banded into stacks of a hundred. The stacks are packaged into "bricks" of four thousand bills each. The bricks are put in pouches for shipment to one of the Federal Reserve banks.

Counterfeiting

Counterfeit coins are less of a problem than counterfeit notes. The Treasury Department has developed ways to make counterfeiting difficult. Each engraver

COUNTERFEITERS

Where do counterfeiters come from? They can be from any walk of life. One man from Missouri made $15,000 in counterfeit $10 bills. Yet he had not finished eighth grade.

Counterfeiters hire people to help them pass off fake currency. One way is for a group of money passers to work together. They go into stores at busy periods. They pay for a few dollars' worth of merchandise using a fifty-dollar bill. They get their change in real money. By the time someone notices the counterfeit money, the people who have passed it are many miles away. Agents of the U.S. Secret Service work hard to catch counterfeiters.

The largest counterfeit ring in history was organized by the Nazis during World War II. Adolf Hitler ordered more than $630 million of counterfeit British currency to be made. Men and women began passing this money all over Britain and in other countries where British money was accepted. Hitler hoped that other countries would lose confidence in the British economy. He also wanted to confuse the British people, so that they would lose faith in their government. Hitler believed this would help Germany gain power over Great Britain. However, Germany was defeated before the Nazi plan could succeed.

has his or her own special style, which is difficult to copy. Just as it is hard to copy someone's signature, it is hard to copy exactly the style of each engraver. Currency paper is of higher quality than most other paper. The green ink used is especially difficult to photograph. The shading does not come out clearly, which makes it hard for a counterfeiter to copy.

Modern counterfeiters use laser printers and color copiers to make illegal copies of notes. But the

Treasury Department has developed new ways to protect money.

In one method, colored polyester threads with the initials USA, the bill's denomination, and a flag are woven into the bill next to the portrait. Polyester thread cannot be copied on a color copier. If you hold such a bill up to the light, you can see these threads. You will not be able to see them in a counterfeit bill.

In another method, tiny microprinted words appear in two places on the front of each bill. The letters are designed to be too small to be copied clearly by a photocopy machine.

Other ways to prevent counterfeiting include a new color-shifting ink. It changes from green to black when viewed from different angles. Also, the portraits on bills are now printed slightly off center.

These measures were added to new bills printed beginning in 1996. All denominations of currency will have security features, except for $1 bills, which are not usually worth counterfeiting. The $20, $50, and $100 bills will have more features, because they are more likely to be copied.

CHAPTER

5

CIRCULATING AND COLLECTING OUR CURRENCY

The Treasury Department ships new paper money and coins to the Federal Reserve banks. The Reserve banks pay it out to commercial banks and savings and loan associations. People get money when they cash checks or withdraw money at their banks. They then spend the money, which is redeposited in banks.

Congress passes laws about the maximum amount of money that can be in circulation at any one time. The Federal Reserve System supervises the flow of money. The president of the United States appoints seven governors of the Federal Reserve Board. They serve for fourteen years. In this way, they can make money decisions that will be good for the country for a long time.

Opposite:
As money circulates, it becomes worn. The average $1 bill lasts only about eighteen months.

When Money Wears Out

As money circulates, it wears out or becomes damaged. The average $1 bill, for example, lasts fifteen to eighteen months. Larger denominations last longer, because they do not circulate as much as the $1 bill. A $20 bill lasts four years, while a $50 bill lasts nine years. Coins last much longer than paper money. Most circulate for thirty years.

What should you do if you receive a torn bill? Is it still worth its original value? A bank will give you an undamaged bill for a torn one. But it must be clearly more than one-half of the original note.

The bank then sends your torn bill to a Federal Reserve bank, along with any other damaged money it has collected. The Federal Reserve bank counts the damaged money. It decides if it is "fit" or "unfit" for use. Fit (reusable) money is stored in vaults until it is needed. Unfit currency is destroyed. Damaged and worn coins are returned to the Treasury Department. They are melted down and made into new coins.

What happens if the note is so badly damaged that you cannot tell what it is? What if you have less than half of the bill? Then you have what is known as mutilated currency. Sometimes mutilated currency has been damaged by chemicals, fire, or explosives. Sometimes insects eat parts of it.

Alan Greenspan has been an influential chairman of the Federal Reserve Board since the 1980s.

ROB THE MINT?

The Denver Mint seems like a tempting target for robbery. It is a storehouse for tons of coins. More than 50 million ounces in gold bars are stored deep below the Mint. The gold belongs to the United States government and is never sold or used.

Security is tight. Visitors must be X-rayed by equipment similar to that at airports. Employees are not allowed to bring coins into the building. They must use special credit cards to operate the vending machines. All workers are X-rayed when they leave the building.

Gold has been stolen just once in the Mint's history. In 1926, an employee with an artificial leg smuggled out $80,000 worth of small gold bars in his hollow limb.

He was caught and sent to prison. Security in the Mint was tightened.

The largest theft took place in front of the Mint, not inside it. It is known as the Great Mint Robbery. It took place on December 18, 1922. Brand new, crisp $5 bills—$200,000 worth—were being transferred from the Mint into a Federal Reserve bank car. Four bandits with sawed-off shotguns grabbed the money bags. One guard was killed. Twenty-seven days later the getaway car was found locked in a garage near the center of Denver. In the front seat was the frozen body of one of the gang members. He had been shot during the robbery. No further evidence was found and no one was ever charged with the crime.

Mutilated currency must be sent to the U.S. Treasury Department. Experts there decide how much it is worth. They redeem the mutilated currency. This means they mail checks back to the people who sent in the damaged money. Every year the Treasury redeems more than $30 million of mutilated currency.

The Fun of Numismatics

The study or collection of coins and paper money is called numismatics. Many people enjoy collecting rare coins or bills. "Mistakes" in the printing or coining process become valued collectors' items.

Each year the mint produces "proof" coins for collectors. Proof coins are made shinier than regular ones by a special polishing process. They are then sealed in plastic.

COLLECTING CURRENCY

If you are interested in learning more about collecting currency, look in your telephone book under "Hobbies" or "Coins." To get ordering information for U.S. Mint coins and medals contact:

Customer Service Center
United States Mint
10001 Aerospace Drive
Lanham, Maryland 20706
(301)436-7400
www.usmint.gov/

The Bicentennial Coin of 1976

For more information about collecting special documents and United States paper money contact the Department of the Treasury at:
Public Affairs
Bureau of Engraving and Printing
Department of the Treasury
14th and C Street, NW
Room 602-11A
Washington, D.C. 20228
(202)447-0193
www.moneyfactory.com

Uncirculated mint sets are also packaged each year. They include one of each denomination of coin. Unlike proofs, they are ordinary coins. They have not been specially polished.

From time to time, the Mint produces special coins in honor of historical events or to honor a famous person. The first commemorative coin was minted in 1892 to help finance the World's Columbian Exposition in Chicago. Since that time, the Mint has issued many commemorative coins. They sell for more than the face value, so they rarely circulate. But they are legal tender.

The Mint also produces commemorative medals. They honor famous people in our country's history. For example, there are bronze medals honoring each American president.

The Bureau of Engraving and Printing also has a mail order sales division. It sells items such as uncut sheets of currency and presidential portraits.

Collecting coins tends to be more popular than collecting paper money. The value of the coins depends on their condition. Proof coins or uncirculated sets are worth more than worn coins. The fewer coins of a given type that are minted, the more each one of them is worth. Older coins tend to be worth more than recent issues. For example, the first coins struck at the Mint were silver half cents. Some of them are valued at more than $20,000. Mistakes in printing also raise the value. The 1937 three-legged buffalo nickels are worth $80 to $16,500. Ordinary 1937 nickels are valued at 30 cents to $25.

The Value of Money Today

Thousands of years ago, people could get along without money. They lived on the food they grew and the things they got by bartering. Today the world is very different. We depend on money.

Imagine what would happen if suddenly there were no money. Stores would close. Cars and trains and airplanes couldn't operate. People who lived on farms could at least feed themselves for a while. But how would they buy seeds or animals without money?

Still, some people think there will be no need for money in the future. Transfers of money can already be done electronically using computers. Electronic bank tellers and facsimile (FAX) machines will carry on more bank business in the future. Purchases will be done with credit cards or checks. Bills or coins won't be needed.

It is hard to predict how our money system might change in the future. However, we can be sure that the Treasury Department will respond to a need for change. In the past, the Treasury has adapted money to fit our needs. That is why some types of currency are no longer used. We now have plenty of coins, so there's no need for fractional currency. When gold and silver each became more scarce, gold and silver certificates were no longer issued. Large-sized bills were replaced by the modern-sized paper currency in 1929. This might sound like a lot of changes, but actually it's not. United States money has been changed the least of any major currency in the world.

The first American money was designed to show our independence from Britain. Then, American leaders worked hard to plan a strong currency system. Today, Congress and the Federal Reserve Board control the amount of money that can be circulated. If the amount in circulation were suddenly doubled, that would mean that the value of the dollar would drop a great deal. The Federal Reserve Board continues as our "money doctor," watching to see when banks need more currency and when they need less. In this way, all American citizens and their money are protected.

In Germany, after World War I, the German mark became worthless. Citizens were forced to carry baskets full of money to buy simple items.

Chronology

700 B.C. Earliest known coins made in Asia Minor (modern-day Turkey) by people of a region called Lydia.

1652 The Massachusetts Bay Colony opens a mint in Boston, making the Pine Tree Shilling until 1686.

1775 American paper money, called Continental Currency, first appears.

1787 The first national coins, made of copper, are introduced.

1789 Alexander Hamilton is appointed the first secretary of the Treasury.

1792 Congress passes the Coinage Act, adopting the dollar as the standard monetary unit.

1792 David Rittenhouse is appointed the first director of the U.S. Mint.

1865 The government begins printing gold certificates.

1878 The first silver certificates are issued.

1968 Circulation of silver certificates ends.

1970 Silver is eliminated from newly minted coins due to worldwide shortages.

1984 The motto "In God We Trust" appears for the first time on all U.S. coins.

1999 The Mint issues the first five 50 State Quarters. Every year until 2008, five new quarters will be issued in the order that the states joined the Union.

2000 The Sacagawea Golden Dollar is released.

For Further Reading

Dunnan, Nancy. *Banking*. Englewood Cliffs, NJ: Silver Burdett Press, 1990.

Godfrey, Neale S. *Ultimate Kids' Money Book*. New York: Simon & Schuster Children's Books, 1998.

Lewis, Brenda Ralph. *Coins & Currency*. New York: Random House, 1993.

Maestro, Betsy C. *The Story of Money*. New York: Houghton Mifflin Company, 1993.

O'Toole, Thomas. *The Economic History of the United States*. Minneapolis: Lerner Publications, 1990.

Sandak, Cass R. *The National Debt*. Brookfield, CT: Twenty-First Century Books, Inc. (Millbrook Press), 1996.

Schlesinger, Arthur M., Jr., ed. *The Department of the Treasury*. Broomall, PA: Chelsea House, 1990.

———, ed. *The Federal Reserve System*. Broomall, PA: Chelsea House, 1990.

Thoren, Margaret. *Figuring Out the Fed*. Chagrin Falls, Ohio: Truth in Money, 1993.

Young, Robert. *Money*. Minneapolis: The Lerner Publishing Group, 1998.

Web Sites

Bureau of Engraving and Printing
<http://www.moneyfactory.com>

U.S. Mint
<http://www.usmint.gov/>

Department of the Treasury
<http://www.treas.gov/>

Federal Reserve System
<http://www.nyfrb.org.links.html>

Index